The Day the Wishing Well Went Dry

Level 9 – Gold

Helpful Hints for Reading at Home

The graphemes (written letters) and phonemes (units of sound) used throughout this series are aligned with Letters and Sounds. This offers a consistent approach to learning whether reading at home or in the classroom.

HERE ARE SOME COMMON WORDS THAT YOUR CHILD MIGHT FIND TRICKY:

water	where	would	know	thought	through	couldn't
laughed	eyes	once	we're	school	can't	our

TOP TIPS FOR HELPING YOUR CHILD TO READ:

- Encourage your child to read aloud as well as silently to themselves.
- Allow your child time to absorb the text and make comments.
- Ask simple questions about the text to assess understanding.
- Encourage your child to clarify the meaning of new vocabulary.

This book focuses on developing independence, fluency and comprehension. It is a gold level 9 book band.

The Day the Wishing Well Went Dry

Written by
Charis Mather

Illustrated by
Lynne Feng

Behind a quiet village nestled in a silver birch forest, there was once an old wishing well where all the birds in the woods met to sing. The wishing well had tufts of the brightest green moss sprouting from between its smooth stones, and a pool of cool water at the bottom.

Every morning, as the sunlight peeked through the trees, a little girl would make her way from the village to perch on the edge of the well.

On her way, the girl would always stop to pick up a small stone and put it in her pouch.

The birds gathered round the girl each morning to hear her wish. She would take a stone from her pouch, close her eyes, and drop it into the well, listening closely for the gentle splash as it met the water.

"What have you wished for today?" the birds would ask.

The little girl always replied the same: "Today, kind birds, I have wished for a little sun for the flowers, and a little rain for the rivers."

When her wish was made, she would skip back home with an empty pouch.

One day, as the young girl was choosing the perfect stone, she saw an old woman with slumped shoulders on the path, a wicker basket at her feet.

"Dear grandmother," the girl called out. "Why do you look so sad?"

"Sweet child," the old woman replied, "I have dropped my basket of herbs and they have scattered everywhere. I am too old to stoop down to reach them, and I fear the wind will whisk them away."

"How terrible!" said the girl. "But I am young and fast – I will catch the herbs before the wind can steal them."

And so she did, running to and fro until the basket was filled once again. When she was done, the girl crouched down to find just the right stone and showed it to the old woman.

"Dear grandmother, today and every day after I shall make a wish for you in the well, that tomorrow your feet will be steady and the breeze gentle," said the girl. "Then, you need not fear for tripping on a rock and spilling your basket."

The woman thanked the girl with a smile and carried on her way.

The girl skipped into the woods to sit by the well once more, this time with two wishes weighing down her pouch. She listened for one splash... then another.

"What have you wished for today?" sang the little birds, seeing she had brought two stones.

"Kind birds", she said, "today, I have wished for a little sun for the flowers, and a little rain for the rivers. I wished also for the old woman on the path, that she will have steady feet and a gentle breeze."

The next morning, the little girl went down to the stream to choose two stones. On her way, she saw a rosy-faced farmer peering into a thicket.

"Good farmer," she called out to him. "Why do you look so worried?"

"Young one," the farmer replied with a frown, "my little lamb has run off the trail and has caught itself in a bramble bush, but I am too big and tall to reach it under the thorns."

"How terrible!" said the girl. "But I am small and nimble. I will crawl into the thicket and free your lamb."

"You must be careful," said the farmer. "The thorns are very sharp."

But the little girl did not mind the thorns as they bit her arms. She ducked into the thicket and pulled the young lamb's soft coat free.

When the lamb was safe, the girl showed the farmer a small stone from under the bush.

"Good farmer, today and every day after I shall make a wish for you in the well, that tomorrow your lamb will stay close by your side so it will not be caught again."

The farmer thanked the girl and carried on his way.

When the little girl had chosen all three stones for the wishing well, she skipped back into the woods. As she made her wishes, she listened for one splash... then another... then another.

"What have you wished for today?" sang the little birds, seeing she had brought three stones.

"Kind birds," she said, "today, I have wished for a little sun for the flowers, and a little rain for the rivers. I wished also for the old woman on the path, and for the good farmer and his lamb, that it will not stray and catch its soft wool in the brambles."

Day after day, the girl would visit the well to make her wishes. Every morning, she would choose the right stones and drop them down one by one. Whenever she met someone in need, she would always stop to help and promise them a wish.

The birds watched as she made more and more wishes for the people in the village. They began to worry for the selfless girl as her feet grew heavier with every new wish.

Before long, she had so many wishes to make that she could not fit all of the stones in her pouch.

One day, as she listened at the edge of the well, the little girl heard something very unusual. Today, not one of her wishes had made a splash. Instead, there was quiet clatter as the stones fell to the bottom of the wishing well.

"Oh birds," she cried out when they asked what she had wished for, "something terrible has happened. Today I have not made even a single wish, as the well has run out. I shall no longer be able to help all the friends I have made in the village."

Seeing the girl's distress, but not knowing how to help, the little birds flocked to the village. There, they met the farmer and the old woman whom the girl had cast wishes for so many times.

"Good farmer, dear grandmother," they chirped, "you must come and help. Our kind friend is very sad, for her wishing well has run dry, and she does not know what to do."

And so, the farmer and the woman followed the birds to the well, taking with them the woman's basket and a ladder from the villagers.

They found the girl sitting sadly next to the well.

"Cheer up, little one," the birds sang to her. "Your friends have come to fix the well."

The old woman put her arm around the girl. "You have helped all of us – now we get to help you," she said.

The farmer lowered the ladder into the well and climbed down. A short while later, he lifted the basket out, now heavy with all the rocks that the little girl had thrown in.

"There," he said. "It was only some stones that had clogged up the well."

"How kind of you," she said, feeling grateful. "I must return the kindness somehow. Only, I cannot make a wish, or the well will dry up again."

"Look how much kindness you have already given," said the woman. "Enough to fill a basket! What need is there for wishes when there are such kind girls as you?"

"Your kindness is worth a thousand wishes," agreed the farmer.

At this, the girl's heart lifted. Watching from above, the birds sang joyfully as the little girl skipped home with the brightest smile and the lightest feet she'd had in a long time.

The Day the Wishing Well Went Dry

1. What caused the well to be blocked?
   a) Stones
   b) Leaves
   c) Moss

2. What is a wish? Have you ever made a wish?

3. Who was the first person the girl made a wish for?

4. How did the girl help the farmer?

5. What does it mean to be kind? How does being kind help people?

©2022 **BookLife Publishing Ltd.**
King's Lynn, Norfolk, PE30 4LS, UK

ISBN 978-1-80155-809-9

All rights reserved. Printed in Poland.
A catalogue record for this book is available from the British Library.

The Day the Wishing Well Went Dry
Written by Charis Mather
Illustrated by Lynne Feng

An Introduction to BookLife Readers...

Our Readers have been specifically created in line with the London Institute of Education's approach to book banding and are phonetically decodable and ordered to support each phase of Letters and Sounds.

Each book has been created to provide the best possible reading and learning experience. Our aim is to share our love of books with children, providing both emerging readers and prolific page-turners with beautiful books that are guaranteed to provoke interest and learning, regardless of ability.

BOOK BAND GRADED using the Institute of Education's approach to levelling.

PHONETICALLY DECODABLE supporting each phase of Letters and Sounds.

EXERCISES AND QUESTIONS to offer reinforcement and to ascertain comprehension.

BEAUTIFULLY ILLUSTRATED to inspire and provoke engagement, providing a variety of styles for the reader to enjoy whilst reading through the series.

AUTHOR INSIGHT:
CHARIS MATHER

Charis Mather is a children's author at BookLife Publishing who has a love for writing stories. Charis enjoys both reading and writing about the weird and wonderful, whether from the real world or from the imagination. Her studies in linguistics and experiences working with young readers have given her a knack for writing material that suits a range of ages and skill levels. Charis is passionate about producing books that emphasise the fun in reading and is convinced that no matter how much you already know, there is always something new to learn.

This book focuses on developing independence, fluency and comprehension. It is a gold level 9 book band.